Original title:
The Fish's Tale

Copyright © 2025 Creative Arts Management OÜ
All rights reserved.

Author: Elias Marchant
ISBN HARDBACK: 978-1-80587-276-4
ISBN PAPERBACK: 978-1-80587-746-2

Shadows in Coral Gardens

In coral homes where shadows play,
A crab in slippers starts ballet.
Starfish giggle as they spin,
While seahorses cheer with a fin.

A snail in shades glides with flair,
Waves crash softly, a salty air.
Octopuses juggle with great glee,
In a treasure chest, they hold a spree.

Jellyfish bouncing, a boisterous crowd,
Broadcasting laughter, oh so loud.
Anemones sway as they join the fun,
In this coral dance, we're all number one!

Among the flippers, we twirl and cheer,
In underwater joy, there's nothing to fear.
For every twist and silly spin,
In this watery realm, we all fit in!

Glimmering Dreams Beneath

Bubbles rise in a swirling stream,
Flounders waddle in a silly dream.
Clownfish grin with painted faces,
While snails race through ordinary places.

Seaweed sways to the beat they find,
With a conch-shell DJ, oh so kind.
Dolphins flip in a sudden jest,
Spraying laughter, they never rest.

A starfish sings in a quirky tone,
While helpfully lending a spiny bone.
Glimmers of laughter beneath the waves,
Turn grumpy frowns into joyful braves.

In their frolic, the rays take a spin,
Laughing with friends, they always win.
In every current, their giggles abound,
In this realm, joy is truly found!

Selkie Secrets Revealed

On moonlit rocks, a secret dance,
Selkies prance in a gleeful trance.
With fishy friends, they gather round,
In the laughter of waves, their joy is found.

They wear their skins with cheeky pride,
Wiggling and squirming, they never hide.
Seals in sunglasses make a toast,
To every flip and silly boast!

With seaweed crowns and kelp guitars,
They sing for mermaids and ocean stars.
A splash of foam, a cheeky shout,
As they spin tales of laughter and doubt.

Through giggles and whispers, tales unfold,
With every jest, a memory bold.
Selkies dance under starry skies,
In this world where laughter flies!

Odyssey of the Silver Stream

In a silver stream, the minnows play,
Dodging bubbles and reeds all day.
With wiggles and giggles, they swim so fast,
Creating ripples that surely last.

A wise old turtle, slow and sly,
Watches the minnows as they fly.
He chuckles softly, "Oh what a scene!
You silly fish, you're all so keen!"

A splash from a frog starts a silly chase,
Water flies with every trace.
The fish all giggle, a joyful race,
In this odyssey, they find their place.

They twirl and dart under shining rays,
With leaps and bounds, the fun never stays.
In the stream of laughter, they glide and gleam,
Living their life like a wondrous dream!

Beneath the Boat

A guppy in a bowler hat,
Swims in circles, looking quite fat.
He twirls and spins, what a sight,
Making the oarsmen laugh with delight.

Bubbles rise like little balloons,
As he serenades the passing moons.
With each splash, he starts to dance,
In this watery world, he takes a chance.

A crab joins in, with claws a-clap,
They start a jig, a merry map.
The sailors chuckle, how absurd,
As their lunch turns to laughter, unheard!

Underneath, where the secrets lie,
Fish trade stories, gazing up at the sky.
While above, the humans bicker,
Below, fish waltz, their hearts much thicker.

Currents of Imagination

A daring minnow, quite a thinker,
Wore a mustache made of tinker.
He plotted schemes to catch a snack,
While dodging hooks that humans pack.

With friends in tow, all in disguise,
They swam around with skeptical eyes.
A seahorse dressed up like a knight,
Claiming he'd win, oh what a sight!

They formed a band of playful jest,
Playing hide and seek, oh what a quest!
A clownfish yelled, "Let's switch our tails!"
Echoing laughter blew through the gales.

And when the sun began to set,
They all agreed, "Best day yet!"
For in the depths where silly dwells,
Joy is measured in fishy spells.

Beneath the Rippled Surface

A wriggly worm on a fishing line,
Complained to fish, "This isn't fine!"
"A nibble here, I'll soon be toast,
You'll all enjoy my barbecue boast!"

A puffer fish, with cheeks all puffed,
Laughed out loud, "You've had it tough!"
"Don't mind the fate that waits for you,
Join our party, we'll make a stew!"

With all the fish in the swirling tide,
They danced around, their worries aside.
The worm was torn, but chose to dive,
"To join this feast, I must survive!"

They twisted and twirled, wave after wave,
With jokes and glee, so much to save.
In laughter's embrace, they found delight,
Even wormy woes turned out quite bright.

Echoes of the Deep

An octopus with a funny flair,
Wore socks on legs, a sight so rare!
With arms in motion, they'd twirl and whirl,
Making bubbles, as they'd gracefully swirl.

A sturgeon smiled, "What's the deal?
Where's the party? Give me a meal!"
As jigs and giggles lit up the sea,
All joined in for a splashy jubilee.

The jellyfish glowed with neon pride,
Floating around in the joyful ride.
While sharks just rolled their eyes with glee,
"How silly can fish be?" we all agree!

In every fin, there was laughter spread,
Echoing tunes of joy ahead.
For beneath the waves where tales unfold,
Life was silly, vibrant, and bold!

Undertows of Longing

In the ocean's warm embrace,
A flounder dreamed of outer space.
He swam with glee, a comical sight,
Wishing on stars in the deep of night.

With a crab who danced, a clown on the shore,
Their laughter echoed, they wanted more.
'To the moon,' laughed the fish, 'let's take a ride!'
But they tripped on seaweed, and tumbled wide.

Sagas from the Sea Bed

A turtle told tales that grew each year,
Of treasure hunts and squid with beer.
"I saw a shark who painted his fins,
With stripes of ketchup and mustard spins!"

An octopus joined with eight arms waving,
"Let's start a band; the crowd will be raving!"
But all they played was a bubble-pop tune,
And danced till the dawn, beneath the full moon.

Colorful Journeys Through Coral Reefs

In the reef where colors shine so bright,
A dolphin asked, "What's for dinner tonight?"
"Seaweed spaghetti or clam chowder fun?"
"Just avoid the net; I'm trying to run!"

A parrotfish giggled, "Let's feast and play!
We'll skip all the drama, come what may!"
But a sea urchin grumbled, "I just want peace!"
As they swirled around, laughter wouldn't cease.

The Flicker of Fins in Moonlight

Under the moon, fins flickered with cheer,
A school of fish shared stories unclear.
"Last night, I saw a catfish in shades,
It's the new fashion—stop all the charades!"

One fish proclaimed, "I can swim backward!"
The group burst out laughing, hearts moving faster.
"Let's compete in a race—not too far,
But watch for the bubbles; they'll raise the bar!"

Depths of Enchanted Waters

In a sea of surprise, where laughter does gleam,
Fins tickle the bubbles, creating a dream.
A crab told a joke to a shrimp with a grin,
They rolled with the waves, letting the fun begin.

With seaweed mustaches and starfish with hats,
The octopus danced with a flurry of splats.
The pelicans perched, eyes wide in delight,
As they watched the parade, in the depths of the night.

A turtle named Larry, so wise and so slow,
Told tales that would make even dolphins say, "Whoa!"
But the punchlines got tangled in kelp, oh dear!
We laughed 'til we cried, with no trace of a fear.

So let's dive in the waters, our spirits set free,
In this world of enchantment, come swim, you and me!
With bubbles of laughter and fishy delight,
The depths of this ocean are boundless and bright.

The Riddle of the Rolling Tide

A seahorse pondered, with a curious look,
"What's heavy and scales, yet swims like a brook?"
The jellyfish giggled, its bells bouncing high,
"Is it my cousin's a fish or a pie in the sky?"

They gathered around, both silly and sly,
As clam shells erupted, a raucous goodbye.
Even anemones wiggled, in fits of pure glee,
When a fish told a tale of a lost family tree.

"Oh, tell us more!" said the wave-swept rocks,
"Do they wear fancy socks, or dance in rare flocks?"
The fish gave a wink, said, "It's all quite absurd,
But that's just the joy of this oceanic world!"

So they rolled in the tide, laughing loud, unconfined,
Chasing bubbles of riddles, with giggles intertwined.
The riddle of waterway mischief takes flight,
In this zany abyss, where antics feel right.

Songs in the Coral Shadows

In the coral's embrace, where shadows play tricks,
The clownfish and tangs devised playful clicks.
With a wink and a bubble, they sang their sweet song,
A melody bubbling, where all could belong.

A crab played the drums, with shells in his claw,
While a guppy danced round with a nonsensical flaw.
"Let's swim and let's twirl, let's spin like a fan!
For who needs a plan when you're part of this clan?"

Then out from the shadows, a whale joined the show,
With a voice like a trumpet, the whole ocean did glow.
Each fish broke into laughter, as echoes resounded,
In these coral reflections, their joy truly sounded.

They twirled in formation, a festival fair,
With bubbles of happiness rising through air.
So dive in the colors, let your spirit ignite,
In the songs of the shadows, laughter takes flight.

Whirlpools of Forgotten Lore

In whirlpools that swirl at the bottom of fun,
A treasure of giggles, where jest has begun.
Old tales of great fish, from ages gone by,
Are told with a wink and a starlit eye.

A pufferfish pondered, "Oh, what's in a tale?
Do we swim or do we float, when we set down our scale?"
The angelfish laughed, spun tales round and round,
"Just duck, flap, and giggle, let joy be profound!"

With currents that carried their chuckles so high,
The sea cucumbers chuckled and rolled in reply.
While oysters would wiggle, their pearls shimmering bright,
Each story a ripple of laughter and light.

So gather your friends 'neath the kelp and the foam,
For every new venture is a chance to call home.
In whirlpools of humor, where giggles explode,
The ocean's old secrets forever unfold.

The Ocean's Storyteller

In the depths where bubbles rise,
A clam tells tales, much to our surprise.
With pearls of wisdom, he plays his part,
Cracking jokes that warm the heart.

A turtle winks, he's seen it all,
Adventures grand, both big and small.
With every wave, they splash and cheer,
Oh, to be a fish, just swim and steer!

Shimmering Hues

A goldfish sparkles, wearing a crown,
While juggling seashells, he won't back down.
His clownish antics make others laugh,
As he swims around on a rainbow path.

An octopus twirls in a two-step dance,
With eight flailing limbs, he takes a chance.
He slips on a rock, oh what a sight!
In the watery disco, all are alight!

Woven Through Currents

In tangled weeds, a tale unfolds,
Of a wise old crab who never grows old.
He tells of treasures with a goofy grin,
And tips on avoiding the sea's errant fin.

A stingray zips, with a laughter so bright,
He swears the sun always shines at night.
In ocean classrooms, they crack up the class,
As tricksters sneak by, with tricksy sass.

Legends of Lost Reef

In the reef where shadows flicker and wave,
A legend stirs, but the truth's hard to save.
Fish dress in costumes for the annual show,
With glitter and glam, they steal the flow.

The sea urchin spins, the crowd goes wild,
While a barracuda acts like a child.
In this underwater carnival, all's fair,
Where laughter and bubbles dance in the air!

Reflections of a Deep Blue Heart

In the sea of silly dreams,
A fish with big, bright beams.
He wiggles and he jigs about,
Spreading laughter, no doubt!

With a splash and a goofy grin,
He dances to the waves' din.
Tales of clams that sing out loud,
He makes them laugh, oh so proud!

Jellyfish flip like they've got style,
Calling out in a wobbly pile.
"Join us, friend! We're here for fun!"
Bouncing rays beneath the sun!

In this world of finned delight,
Every day's a silly sight.
With friends that giggle and play,
In their hearts, joy leads the way!

The Ocean's Mosaic

Bubbles rise like giggly thoughts,
In a world where humor's caught.
Crabs cracking jokes on the sand,
As the seahorses form a band!

A turtle's shell, a funny hat,
Says, "I'm cool, just look at that!"
Fish with shades drift on by,
"Why the long face?" they always cry.

An octopus with seven arms,
Telling stories, laughing charms.
"Did you hear about the reef?
It made me giggle with its grief!"

Undersea pranks that never end,
Where every creature is a friend.
In the depths where chuckles sway,
Joyful echoes guide the way!

Legends of the Briny Deep

Deep below, where laughter flows,
A fish named Finn, in fun, he grows.
With splashes of joy from all around,
Creating giggles from the ground!

Guppies gather, telling tales,
Of underwater vending sales.
"Buy a joke!" they keenly shout,
The pufferfish laughs, "What's it about?"

In a seaweed maze, they play hide and seek,
Sardines giggle, crazy and sleek.
"Best swimmer wins a crown of shells!"
As the dolphin jokes, oh, how it swells!

With each wave, a smile grows wide,
An ocean of chuckles, no need to hide.
With legends spun in a breezy sweep,
Beneath the waves, it's a world of peep!

Undersea Echoes

In the depths where bubbles burst,
Fish share jokes, they seem rehearsed.
A clownfish wiggles with delight,
His funny face, a joyous sight!

An eel with puns, oh what a tease,
Zig-zags by with evident ease.
"Why did the crab cross the floor?
To get to the shellfish store!"

Mirthful rays of sunlight beam,
As creatures dance, a colorful dream.
The tide sways with giggles bright,
Their laughter floats, a pure delight!

With every wave that comes to pass,
Friendship blooms like soft sea grass.
In the echo of the ocean blue,
A funny tale from me to you!

Currents of Time and Tide

In the river where minnows play,
A catfish dreams of a sunlit bay.
With a wiggle and a flip, he claims his fame,
But oh, it's tough with a silly name!

The crabs just chuckle, the turtles grin,
As he splashes and flops, making quite the din.
He dives for the treasure, a lost old shoe,
And thinks it's the crown of a fishy crew!

A bubble of laughter floats by his side,
As minnows tease, "Come swim, take a ride!"
He swirls and he twirls with bubbles so bright,
In the currents of jest, he swims with delight!

With every swish of his fin so bold,
He tells fancy tales that never get old.
In the aquatic world, he's the king, it's true,
With a heart full of giggles, he reigns over blue!

The Color of Water

In the pond so clear, the frogs croak tunes,
While turtles argue about the phases of moons.
A goldfish dreams of a journey to land,
With popcorn clouds at his finny command!

The lily pads laugh, saying, "A splash is near!"
As he leaps from the depths, not showing a fear.
But alas, on a branch, he gets stuck with a plop,
And the dragonflies giggle, "He won't make it, stop!"

With a shimmer of scales and a flip of a tail,
He'll tell all his buddies of his comical fail.
"Next time I'll leap far from leaves of green,
Where the colors of water can hardly be seen!"

But the ripples remind him with chuckling glee,
That the funniest tales are the ones that set free.
So he swims with a grin, in a whirlpool of fun,
In the color of water, where laughter's begun!

Ripples of the Infinite Flute

In a sea of sounds, the fish dance and sway,
With bubbles that pop in a jazzy array.
An octopus plays on an underwater flute,
While the starfish tap-dance in their funny suit!

The seaweed sways to a whimsical tune,
As crabs join in, under the light of the moon.
"Let's throw a party!" the clownfish declare,
With jellyfish lights floating high in the air!

They shimmy and giggle in currents so bright,
As the rhythm of water twirls through the night.
With melodies wrapped in a splashy embrace,
Their laughter resounds in this underwater space!

In the ripples of joy, friendships bloom and take flight,
With fins swishing tales of their wacky delight.
So join in the fun, let the bubbles inflate,
For in watery realms, there's no room for fate!

The Unseen Journey of Souls

Beneath the surface where shadows play,
The fish gather 'round for a tale each day.
"Once I swam through a whirlpool wide,
And saw all my friends in a dreamlike slide!"

A guppy giggles, "Tell us what you found!"
As the eel weaves stories of journeys profound.
"I met a mermaid who showed me her comb,
Together we danced, far away from home!"

But then comes a whirl, the stories collide,
And the sardines bubble, "Let's take it in stride!"
Bubble-blowing fish say, "What if we fly?
To the clouds above, where the jellyfish cry!"

So they flip through the sea with whimsical grace,
Painting bright pictures in this underwater space.
The unseen journey, a dance so sublime,
Where laughter is timeless, and joy knows no time!

Whispers from the Tide

Once a fish wore a silly hat,
He swam past the octopus, who laughed at that.
Fins flapping wildly, he twirled with glee,
Bubbles popping like a loud cup of tea.

Under the sea, the crabs did a jig,
While seaweed swayed, looking rather big.
A starfish giggled, its arms stretched wide,
As they all danced in a watery slide.

A turtle with shades floated on by,
Said, "Why wear a hat? Just let those fins fly!"
The fish grinned wide, flashing shiny scales,
As seahorses joined in with playful tales.

So if you're ever near a bubbly spree,
Just listen closely, you might hear with glee,
The tales of the sea with a twist so bright,
Where laughter and fun are always in sight.

The Secrets of Saltwater Dreams

In a sea so blue, with dreams all around,
A clam kept a secret, never made a sound.
Though fish swam by with curious looks,
The clam just winked, reading its books.

An anglerfish grinned with an odd little light,
Said, "Let's spill the beans, keep it fun tonight!"
With a wink and a nudge, they gathered near,
And shared all the laughs, with fins full of cheer.

"Did you hear of the turtle who topped the race?
He just took a nap, it's a tired old case!"
The ocean laughed out loud, from reef to bay,
As the mussels chimed in, "Hey, what do you say?"

So gather 'round, let's unleash these dreams,
The salty tales swim in giggles and beams.
For underneath the waves, together we'll beam,
In a world made of laughter, and oceanic dreams.

A Dance Beneath the Waves

At twilight's dance, the starfish did prance,
With swirls and twirls, they led the romance.
Fish joined the beat, in a shimmering race,
Creating a whirlpool, each wore a face.

A pufferfish puffed to the sound of a beat,
And jellyfish glided, so light on their feet.
"Watch out for the shrimp!" called a whale with a grin,
As they all spun around in a tide of fun spins.

An old grouper joked, "What's the dance if you miss?
Don't worry, my friends, it's a splashy abyss!"
So wave after wave, the creatures took flight,
Beneath the blue moon, they danced with delight.

Through bubbles and laughter, their spirits alive,
They twirled 'neath the tide, feeling joyfully thrive.
In the ocean's embrace, with giggles galore,
Dancing dreams intertwined on the ocean floor.

Siren's Call of the Ocean

From rock to rock, the mermaids would sing,
Chasing caught laughs in the tide's playful swing.
"Come join the fun!" they'd merrily call,
And the fish all cheered from their watery hall.

With shimmer and sparkle, they danced on the sand,
Their whimsical tunes made the sea creatures band.
A lighthearted sea bass, quite sharp in the mind,
Said, "I'll be your DJ; let's make it unwind!"

The crabs formed a circle, doing the twist,
While cozy sea sponges bobbed to the mist.
"Hey, what's the catch?" a nearby seagull cried,
"Just jelly and laughter, come jump in the tide!"

As night fell softly, with a wink and a hum,
The sea echoed with joy, and the party got numb.
So listen closely, whenever they call,
The siren's sweet laugh is a tale for us all.

Navigating the Liquid Labyrinth

In waters deep, a tale began,
A fish in hat, with great big plans.
It swam through seaweed, oh so bright,
Wearing a smile, what a funny sight!

With a wink and grin, it dashed away,
Dodging bubbles at splashy play.
It found a crab, who danced nearby,
Together they laughed, oh my, oh my!

But every turn brought silly slips,
As starfish teased with silly quips.
The seahorse rolled, a giggling fool,
In this wet maze, they made their rule.

So join the fun, take a deep dive,
With laughs and splashes, you'll surely thrive.
In this maze of laughter, no need to pout,
For in each splash, joy's what it's about!

Echoes of Distant Shores

A fish with fins and tales to tell,
Swam by the shore where it liked to dwell.
It found a clam that chirped with glee,
Together they sang, as merry as can be!

From rock to rock, they danced in rhyme,
Crabs joined in with a beat so prime.
The tide joined in with a chuckle loud,
Echoes of laughter, beneath a cloud.

With each little splash, the tales grew big,
As jellyfish twirled in a humorous jig.
They danced and spun, all in a whirl,
Making the sea their joyous pearl.

So listen close, as waves come ashore,
For laughter echoes from sea to more.
In salty musings and ripples that gleam,
You'll find the humor in every dream!

Unraveling the Mystery of the Blue

In the deep where the waters swirl,
Lived a fish who thought it was a pearl.
With fins so flashy, it sought to shine,
Dreaming of fame in the ocean divine.

It snuck past currents, full of flair,
Casting its net with nary a care.
But all it caught were laughs and cheers,
From seaweed buddies and playful peers.

The treasure it sought was not gold,
But moments spent in stories told.
With chuckles exchanged and smiles anew,
The mystery unraveled in shades of blue.

So join the finned ones in their quest,
For humor's the prize that makes it the best.
In depths unseen, where laughter flows,
The joy of the ocean forever glows!

The Sailor's Shadow Beneath

In the sunlit waves, a sailor sat,
His shadow danced with a giggling splat.
The fish below, with a twitchy tail,
Invited the sailor to join its trail.

They played hide and seek in the ocean wide,
With bubbles bursting and fish that glide.
The sailor's laugh echoed off the boat,
As the fish swam close, afloat like a coat.

As seaweed tickled and waves did sway,
They told silly stories to waste the day.
With every splash and joyous sound,
Laughter bubbled up all around.

So if you wander by the coast so free,
Look below for laughter and glee.
Join the sailor and fish in their fun,
For in their shadows, joy has begun!

Beneath the Waves

In the depths where bubbles rise,
A clownfish dons a bright disguise.
He tells a joke to seaweed pals,
They laugh so hard, they start to thralls.

A crab with sass and sideways strut,
Claims he's the king—oh, what a nut!
He waves his claws, so proud and loud,
While dolphins giggle, a silly crowd.

A turtle slow, too cool to care,
Wears sunglasses, oh-so-fair.
He flips his shell toward the sun,
Declares, "Life's a beach, now that's fun!"

With jellyfish dancing in a trance,
They sway and twirl, a liquid dance.
"Who needs a partner?" one does quip,
"I'll just float along with my own flip!"

Whispers of the Deep

Beneath the blue, we gather round,
A seaweed band without a sound.
A puffer fish tries to play the flute,
But all we hear is a 'toot-toot' brute.

An octopus with paintbrush flair,
Creates a mural on seaweed hair.
"Not quite Van Gogh, but cute, I swear!"
The fishes giggle, with no care.

Starfish gossip, do they know?
Who caught the biggest fishy show?
They claim they saw it wriggle fast,
But as usual, tales grow vast!

A seahorse in a tiny shoe,
Struts like he's in a fashion view.
He twirls and sways, a sight to behold,
Says, "Fabulous fins, let's be bold!"

Scales of Secrets

A glimmering scale sings a jest,
About the clam who took a rest.
He snored so loud, the fish all fled,
"Don't disturb the sleepy!" one fish said.

A guppy with a golden dream,
Wonders if he'll win the stream.
He casts a line with silly bait,
"Fishing's fun when you're not late!"

A wise old whale spills tales galore,
Of underwater ocean lore.
He's half asleep, but what a twaddle,
His stories waver, a fishy battle.

With every splash and silly flip,
The ocean chuckles with each trip.
Together they laugh, sing, and sway,
In currents where the shadows play.

Echoes from the Abyss

In the ocean's depths where shadows loom,
Shy squids giggle in their inky room.
They play hide and seek, what a sight,
With bubbles bursting, oh, what delight!

A tangy tuna with a voice so loud,
Sings silly songs to the lounging crowd.
His tunes, they echo through coral halls,
"Come join my concert!" he proudly calls.

A dolphin's prank, he flips and dives,
With a woeful crab, who never thrives.
"Why not just swim?" the crab did sigh,
"Because I'm too busy, oh my, oh my!"

With laughter bubbling from every fin,
They share the joy beneath the skin.
Where every flick and every tale,
Brings a chuckle in the whale's big wail.

Beneath the Scales

In a world where bubbles rise,
A guppy tells a grand surprise.
"I caught a hook that wore a hat,
And danced around a sleeping cat!"

He swirled and twirled beneath the waves,
Incredible tales of watery caves.
"I saw a shell that sang a tune,
While juggling pearls beneath the moon!"

The crabs all laughed, they knew the game,
For fishy tales are never tame.
With fins that flap, they swish about,
And share their truths, without a doubt!

So join the splash and heed the call,
For depths hold stories great and small.
Each ripple brings a new delight,
In the underwater world so bright!

Stories of the Silent Stream

In a stream where shadows play,
A trout has tales to weave each day.
"I once met a snake, quite sly, you see,
Who argued fish should fly like me!"

He laughed so hard that bubbles blew,
And startled all the frogs, it's true.
"A crab claimed he could walk on land,
But slipped and fell, oh wasn't that grand!"

They chatted on till twilight fell,
With funny bits to share, oh swell!
"One day I dodged a fisher's net,
And danced with otters — best day yet!"

So come, sit back, and join the fun,
With tales of fish and friends to run.
In currents where the laughter streams,
There's more to fish than just their dreams!

Currents of Longing

There once swam a lonely bass,
Dreaming of a world to surpass.
"I yearn to dance in shallow pools,
Away from all these common rules!"

He saw a minnow, small and spry,
Doing the jig, oh me, oh my!
"Let's start a band, we'll rock the bay,
And throw a party for the day!"

They twirled 'round rocks, they glided fast,
With bubbles popping, friendships cast.
"A salmon joined, she's quite a star,
And swims like she's the queen, by far!"

Oh, currents pull us here and there,
With laughter shared beyond compare.
In watery depths, their dreams took flight,
And danced till dawn, all through the night!

The Forgotten Lagoon

In a lagoon where lanterns glow,
A couple fish put on a show.
"We've got secrets, no one knows,
Like how to tango on our toes!"

With swirls and spins, they set the scene,
Their fins a blur, oh so serene.
"An eel tried once to join the dance,
But tripped and caused the crowds to prance!"

Then came a crab with clumsy claws,
Who clapped along and took a pause.
"I never knew that fish could sway,
You've taught me how to party play!"

The moonlight sparkled on their scales,
As laughter echoed through the gales.
In the forgotten lagoon so fine,
Fish tell their tales, and brightly shine!

Fragments from a Waterborne Odyssey

Bubbles dance in a slippery waltz,
A seaweed princess lost in her faults.
She tried to sing but forgot all the notes,
As turtles giggled in tiny boats.

A clam with a hat said, "Oh dearie me!"
"My pearls aren't just fancy, they're also quite free!"
The clownfish blushed with a wink and a grin,
While jellyfish twirled in their glowing skin.

An octopus juggled his lunch for a show,
Shrimp laughed so hard they forgot how to row.
But when sharks approached, it was all quite absurd,
They turned tail and fled, not a whisper, nor word.

So if you dip your toes in the bubbling blue,
Remember the tales of fish that you knew.
For under the waves, the laughter's quite grand,
In the whimsical world of the ocean's own band.

Melodies Underneath the Surface

A trumpet fish played quite a sweet tune,
While seahorses pranced under a bright moon.
With shells for the drums, they made quite a show,
Spreading joy in the depths where no one could go.

A crab in a tux tried to dance with great flair,
But tripped on a rock, sent coral everywhere.
The crowd roared with laughter, they clapped and they cheered,
As sea creatures grinned, "Oh, we're all engineers!"

An eel struck a pose in a rock concert style,
With a sea turtle scoffing, "You've lost your green smile!"
And schools of fish swayed to their own silly beats,
Digesting the fun through their tiny fish eats.

So if you're ever staring down at the tide,
Remember the band that swam deep and wide.
The melodies echo and tickle your ears,
In the whimsical depths where nothing else fears.

The Heartbeat of a Silent Abyss

In the dark deep blue where the weird things flip,
A lobster threw shade while he munched on a chip.
The octopus chuckled, "What's getting you down?"
"I'm tired of seaweed, it's turning me brown!"

A snail on a rock tried to hurry along,
But a starfish yelled, "Hey! Take it easy, it's long!"
They formed a parade, with a puffer on lead,
While shrimps put confetti on marine weeds.

Anemones waved like they knew the right groove,
And the anglerfish boasted, "I'm making a move!"
But once the applause turned into mere blinks,
They shuffled away to indulge in their drinks.

So if you wander deep where the sunlight withdraws,
Hear the laughter that echoes from fins and from claws.
For down in the depths, humor swims side by side,
In a heartbeat of bliss where the fun is the tide.

Reflections from a Shell

A hermit crab peeked from his glimmering shell,
Said, "Who's that with dreams of the ocean to tell?"
A fish flopped and floundered, his stories unspooled,
"I tried to swim straight, but I vastly misruled!"

With each little story, they giggled a bit,
As a dolphin swam by, doing acrobatic splits.
The otters rolled over, cracking up on a rock,
"Why can't you all swim like my pet goldfish, Doc?"

The moon shone bright on the shimmering sea,
While a clam yelled, "Hey! Stop using my key!"
The laughter echoed and bounced off the tide,
In a shell, there's a mirror where no secrets hide.

So if you ever spot a reflection or glare,
Remember the laughter that shimmers in there.
Fun tales and giggles from a world so divine,
In the depths of the ocean, where all creatures shine.

Reflections in Water

In the shimmering pond they play,
A frog leaps and shouts hooray!
A fish flips, a splash takes flight,
"I'm the star of this watery sight!"

With shimmering scales, they all compete,
Who can dance on this watery street?
The water's just a disco floor,
Where bubbles pop, and laughter soars!

A turtle's slow, a snail just slips,
"Race me!" yells the fish with flips.
But that's no race; it's quite the joke,
As everyone joins in, almost broke!

With all this fun, they know it's true,
Life's a splash, and joy's the glue.
So here's to friends in the big blue lake,
Where giggles and bubbles make no mistake!

Elegy of the Eel

An eel in the mud, oh what a sight,
He wriggles and squiggles, giving a fright!
He tells everyone he's smooth and cool,
But really, he's just a slippery fool!

With a wink and a slither, he starts to brag,
"I slink through the reeds and I never drag!"
But splashes erupt, and he flops with a yell,
His wiggle dance turns into a swell!

He swore he'd win at the undersea race,
But instead he got tangled – oh what a disgrace!
"Next time I'll glide like a wave, you'll see!"
And everyone giggled, "Just let it be!"

So here lies the tale of a joke from the deep,
Where eels prance and frolic, and slip in a heap.
They learn to just chuckle, then swim with cheer,
For life's just a splash when they're all gathered near!

The Angler's Dream

A fisherman casts from his old wooden boat,
Dreaming of fish, he starts to gloat.
"I'll catch the biggest!" he gives a cry,
But all he catches is a bright blue sky!

He baits his hook with a shiny appeal,
But only a duck says, "What a bad deal!"
The fish swim below, all snug in their beds,
While he waves to the clouds that float overhead!

His bobber goes under, he jumps with a start,
But it's just a log, breaking his heart!
"Tomorrow!" he vows, "I'll outsmart that fish!"
While the fish below just laugh at his wish.

As night falls on water, there's silence on tides,
The angler's dream swims where humor resides.
So he tips his hat to the stars up above,
For sometimes the best catch is a laugh from a dove!

School of Shadows

In the depths of the sea, a school of bright fish,
They dart and they dash, each one in a swish.
"Let's play hide and seek!" one little fish shrieks,
As they wiggle and giggle, hiding in creeks.

One hides in a coral, the other in sand,
"Found you!" cries a guppy, with laughter so grand!
But wait! Here comes the prawn with a dance,
He tickles the fish with mischievous prance!

The shadows all flash, bright colors collide,
As they spin through the water, in friendship they glide.
A teacher fish says, "It's time to unite!"
"Let's make a splash and shine really bright!"

So under the waves, where the sunbeams play,
The school of fish live in fun every day.
With laughter and bubbles, they shimmer and sway,
In the dance of the currents, they've found their own way!

Journey Through Aquatic Realms

In waters bright, the minnows dance,
Their tiny fins in silly prance.
One fish swam low, another high,
Chasing bubbles through the sky.

A shark with shades, so cool and bold,
Told tales of treasure and legends old.
While octopuses played hide and seek,
With eight arms flailing, it looked quite bleak.

The turtle, wise, gave advice in rhyme,
On how to have fun and waste some time.
But every swim turned into a race,
Who knew the ocean had such this pace?

From coral reefs to the sandy floors,
They laughed and sang by the open doors.
In this silly world, with a splash and a twirl,
Fishy friends made each day a whirl!

Odes to Oceanic Souls

There once was a crab, proud of his shell,
He strutted around, oh, what a swell!
But when a wave gave him a shake,
He flipped and flopped with a comic quake.

A guppy snapped selfies, quite the show,
While others swam gently, moving slow.
The seaweed waved and joined the fun,
Tickling fins 'til the day was done.

A dolphin roared with laughter so bright,
As he outswam a jellyfish in flight.
"Oh, what a life!" he squeaked with glee,
"Who knew the sea could be so free?"

With bubbles and giggles, they swam around,
Creating laughter wherever they found.
In this watery realm, so wild and free,
The ocean's song was a giddy spree!

The Depths of Longing

A lonely anglerfish sought a mate,
Wore a bright lure, it was worth the wait.
But every fish that came for light,
Thought he was food and swam in fright!

In a sea of grins, he had a frown,
Wishing for love in his deep, dark gown.
Floors of humor were all around,
Yet here he sat, feeling quite down.

Until a clownfish flashed a smile,
Said, "Hey, buddy, let's swim a while!"
They danced through reefs, played tag with brine,
In the depths of longing, they found sunshine.

So don't judge by looks, don't swim away,
Even the weird can bright up a day.
In the ocean's heart, with a laugh or two,
Sometimes strange friends are the best for you!

In Search of Sheltered Harbors

A penguin waddled, lost at sea,
Searching for a cozy place to be.
Every rock looked like home for a while,
But none had a sign that said, 'Come, stay a while!'

A stingray offered to lend a wing,
"Hop on my back; let's make a spring!"
But oh, they leaped and made a splash,
Instead of calm, they had a crash!

Anemones giggled, "Join our party!"
While seahorses twirled, feeling hearty.
Each harbor sought, each port in vain,
They found delight amidst the playful strain.

Finally, a cozy nook came to view,
With shellfish feasts, oh, what a view!
In the chaos, they found their delight,
In the search for home, they found pure light!

Undersea Ballads of Lost Souls

In a bubble of glee, a clownfish did dance,
He twirled through the waves, not missing a chance.
With a wink and a splash, he would tell a joke,
Leaving the seahorses in fits—a grand poke!

A grouper named Gary wore a silly hat,
He claimed it brought luck, but it just made him fat.
With each swim he took, it would bob and it'd sway,
As he laughed at his friend, who was lost in dismay!

The jellyfish jiggled, all bouncy and bright,
Telling tales of their glory with glowing delight.
But they floated away, too lazy for fun,
While the crabs danced in circles and joked in the sun!

In the end, they all laughed, a comedic parade,
From eels to the minnows, all joined the charade.
With fins all a-flutter, they played in a whirl,
In the ocean's grand ball, not a dream, but a swirl!

Glances Across the Oasis Reef

A starfish with shades lounged upon the fine rock,
He claimed he was wise, yet forgot how to talk.
With a napkin adorned and a plate of seaweed,
He exclaimed, "Oh my! What a lovely snack indeed!"

A pufferfish puffed, thought he'd scare off the sharks,
But they just rolled their eyes, found his tricks not up to par.
With a shimmer and giggle, they swam right on by,
Leaving our pufferfish pouting, oh my, oh my!

The octopus played hide-and-seek with a crab,
But the lobster swore loudly, said, "You've been nabbed!"

With tentacles waving, and claws at the ready,
The laughter erupted—oh, weren't they all heady!

In this watery world, with creatures so bold,
Every face was a smile, with stories retold.
Through the reefs and the tides, friendship did thrive,
In this whimsical realm, all were joyous alive!

Fables of the Kin of the Ocean

A narwhal named Ned fancied himself quite grand,
With a tusk like a horn, he led the parade band.
But the trumpetfish laughed, said "You're just a large tube!"
As they floated in rhythm, a silly sea rube!

A little shrimp shouted from his pulpy old nook,
"I've got all the moves; give my dance a good look!"
But as he twirled 'round, he swirled right off course,
And the snapper just snickered—what a clumsy force!

A flounder called Freddy was stuck in his ways,
Claimed he knew all the trends of the underwater praise.
But his fashion was weird—polka dots plus stripes,
Made all of the sea critters roll into giggles and gripes!

At the core of the reef, laughed the friends in a row,
With tales made of bubbles, making merry, the flow.
For in the heart of the sea, where the sun always shines,
Joy is boundless, like rhymes of sea creatures' designs!

The Guardians of the Wave

A turtle named Tim, with a shell shaped like cheese,
Paddled through waters with effortless ease.
He told tales of battles, of sailors, and clout,
But tripped on a barnacle, flopping about!

An angelfish danced, in colors so bright,
Claiming to be a star, oh, what a delight!
Yet when he tried singing, it was quite a mess,
The seaweed just shivered—"Oh, please, try to rest!"

A sea snail, quite slow, dreamed of speedy fame,
Declared he'd outrun the tides, but, alas, what a shame!
As he inched through the sand, feeling quite like a champ,

He reached the end of the beach, cried, "Where's all the stamp?"

Through each wave and bubble, the laughter did glide,
As each tale unwound with a joyous, wild ride.
For in this vast ocean, full of giggles and cheer,
The guardians do play, in a world full of dear!

A Dance in the Wake

In the splash and the sway, there's a jig,
With fins that are flapping like a wild gig.
The bubbles are bursting with giggles galore,
As fish twist and twirl on the ocean's floor.

They spin with a sip of the salty brine,
Wiggling their tails in a line so fine.
A crab joins the beat with a clunky clack,
A dance in the wake, oh, what a whack!

The octopus hops on a seaweed stage,
Drawing in laughter with each quirky page.
A seahorse darts in, with a comical frown,
Twirling and whirling, then tumbling down.

And when the sea turtle joins in the fun,
He moves like a turtle but thinks he's a pun.
With laughter that echoes, they dance 'til late,
In the deep blue expanse, it's a party fate.

Netting the Past

Old nets hang on coral as relics of yore,
Tangled in stories from ocean's floor.
A crab shakes a leg, with a wink and a grin,
Remembering days when his dance was in.

A fish with a mustache swims by with a flair,
He's got tales to tell, if you dare to care.
"Once I caught wind of a whale's really fine
Dinner party feast that I almost declined!"

But the anchovy laughs; "You're just fishin' for fame!
Tales turn as we swim, it's all part of the game!"
With gills all a-flutter, they summon a crowd,
Sharing their tales, and they're really quite loud.

Oh, netting the past is a finny delight,
With stories and laughter that dance in the light.
Each fish has a quirk, unique as they swim,
In a bubbling ocean where tales never dim.

Waters of Whimsy

In the waters of whimsy, the fish spin around,
Telling tall tales that are oddly profound.
A dolphin drops in, sporting shades of bright,
Claiming he danced with a mermaid last night.

The seahorse scoffs, "That's a storyline grand!
You know that they won't even touch your fine hand!"
With laughter like ripples, they gather and jest,
And share secret tales of their oceanic quest.

A goldfish chimes in, "Can you keep a hook?
I once read a story in a washed-up book!"
The fish all burst out in a riot of giggles,
Imitating sharks and their wiggly wiggles.

In this playful ballet where the currents compose,
A symphony bright where the laughter just flows.
Each fin, each bubble, a whimsical note,
In the waters of whimsy, they endlessly float.

Forgotten Depths

In the forgotten depths where the shadows crawl,
The fish often gather to tell tales tall.
With a wink and a swish, they pull from the sea,
"When the waves went to sleep, I was prized as a key!"

A pufferfish puffs, "I once startled a cat,
With a flick of my fin; oh, imagine that!"
They chuckle and chortle, their laughter it swells,
As they share every tale that the deep ocean tells.

A clam chips in, sounding odd and aloof,
"Just the other day, I found out I'm proof—
That pearls can be funny, if you give them a chance,
I winked at a starfish, and it started to dance!"

In these forgotten depths, where the murkiness stays,
They find joy in the quirks of the oceanic maze.
With tales rich in humor, they float and create,
A tale of their own that's just honestly great.

A Glimmer in the Depths

In the ocean, where bubbles rise,
A fish does dance, with sparkly eyes.
It twirls and flips, a merry sight,
Chasing its snack, in pure delight.

With laughter loud, it swirls around,
Tickling octopuses, so profound.
A crab joins in, with a pinch and snap,
In this underwater, joyous slap.

A turtle laughs, in slow-motion jest,
Watching the fish, it's quite impressed.
They play a game, hide and seek enthralled,
In the grassy beds, they're all recalled.

But then a net, it drops from above,
With a splash so loud, it fits like a glove.
"Oh no!" they call, in a funny sprout,
As fishy friends, they wiggle about.

Beneath the Surface

Deep below where eels like to slide,
A fish spins tales of its wild ride.
With bubbles popping, laughter erupts,
As each fin dances, and each tail jumps.

"Have you heard of the whale's big joke?
He tried to sing, but just made smoke!"
The clownfish giggles, with glee in his heart,
Shooting sassy lines, he's the funny part.

A shark swims by, but oh what a fuss,
"I only bite when they're late for a bus!"
Shrimps chuckle low, as they scuttle away,
While seaweed sways, and the crabs start to play.

With coral as stage, the drama unfolds,
A starfish recites as the story is told.
In this watery realm, where the humor's grand,
Every fish shares its tales, all planned.

The Mermaid's Muse

A mermaid sings, in bubbles and foam,
Her fishy friends all make her feel home.
With tails a-flutter, they gather around,
In a chorus of giggles, they leap to the sound.

"Hey, have you seen the seal's new hat?"
"It's made of kelp! How about that?"
The fish roll their eyes, in playful disdain,
As laughter erupts, like a sweet summer rain.

A dolphin jumps, for the comedic burst,
"Try to catch me, I'm going to thirst!"
The fish dart away, with a flurry and dash,
But end up in bubbles, creating a splash.

With seaweed wigs and playful pranks,
They bob in the current, filling the banks.
A crazy parade, as joy fills the sea,
In this whimsical tale, forever carefree.

Luminous Lures

In the deep blue, where lanternfish glow,
A fish wears a hat made of sea-salt snow.
With a wink and a grin, it struts through the tide,
Inviting all critters to join for a ride.

A shrimp suggests, "Let's dance on the reef!"
But a crab yells back, "I'm looking for beef!"
The antics unfold, as they twist and twirl,
Ocean friendships in a salty whirl.

"Check out my moves, I'm quite the catch!"
Said one little fish, with a glittery patch.
They spin and they flick, with scales that mesmerize,
While jellyfish giggle, in colorful ties.

With laughter so bright, it echoes the sea,
These lures of light bring joy, can't you see?
In this underwater ball, they jump and they cheer,
A funny fish tale that's made up of cheer.

Journey of a Silver Fin

A silver fin with dreams so wide,
Swam to dance, not to hide.
He twirled with crabs, made them laugh,
A jellyfish joined, and what a gaffe!

With bubbles blown and wiggles galore,
They spun in circles, then fell to the floor.
The octopus giggled, quite out of breath,
Their cheerful chaos brought joy, not death.

In the shallows, they found a shell,
Inside, a treasure — a shiny bell.
They rang it loud, oh what a sound,
Bringing all creatures to gather around.

So off they went, dancing anew,
In the sea memories like bubbles flew.
With giggles and splashes, they made a team,
A silver fin's life is a glittering dream.

Currents of Memory

In currents swift where fishes play,
A blubbery bass sings night and day.
He croaks his tunes to a dolphin's groove,
To move their fins, oh how they move!

A pufferfish puffed, all big and round,
Scared a young clownfish, who fell to the ground.
But up he popped with a cute little grin,
Saying, "Come on, buddy, let's dive right in!"

Together they floated, bright and bold,
Trading their stories, treasures untold.
A starfish listened, all full of glee,
"Oh, what a world, it's fun to be free!"

With splashes of joy from dusk till noon,
They found laughter's echo from sunken maroon.
In depths so deep, where bubbles rise,
The ocean held secrets wrapped in disguise.

The Ocean's Chronicles

In the azure deep, under waves so bright,
A wise old turtle tells tales at night.
He speaks of fish with hats oh so grand,
And a crab that tap dances on golden sand.

With a wink and a nod, he'd start a rhyme,
His friends all gathered, it was that time.
"A seahorse rode a shark with style,
And they rode through currents for quite a while!"

The tales kept flowing, as bubbles burst,
And starry-eyed fishes listened first.
From laughter to splashes, they all agreed,
Every old story is just what they need.

With a splash from a wave and a flip of a fin,
The ocean's humor draws everyone in.
In watery worlds where giggles thrive,
Chronicles of laughter keep dreams alive.

Tales of the Tides

When tides come rolling, a surprise awaits,
A fish in a costume, oh how it prates!
With sequins shimmering and a feathered hat,
He twirled and laughed, just like that!

Crabs gave a clap with their tiny claws,
While seahorses smiled, simply because.
A silly old octopus joined in the play,
Making funny faces throughout the day.

They formed a line, a parade of sorts,
With a sea star leading, full of quirk and snorts.
They danced on the sand, spun in delight,
Telling tall tales that echoed through night.

At the break of dawn, their laughter would ring,
A chorus of joy, oh what joy they bring!
For in every wave that rolls to the shore,
Lie tales of the tides, we can't help but adore!

Waters of Wonder

In the splash of the tide, fish dance with glee,
They wear tiny hats, sipping tea by the sea.
Giggling bubbles float up to the sky,
While seagulls overhear, and they wonder why.

A crab with a top hat waltzes with grace,
While octopuses juggle in this funny place.
The seaweed sways, it joins the parade,
In this underwater realm, all worries fade.

With a sunfish who dreams of a starry night,
He throws fishy parties with disco lights bright.
Their dance makes the waves laugh and clap,
As barnacles tap to the music's happy rap.

So if you dive deep, chuckle with delight,
For in these waters, there's always a sight.
The ocean's a stage, with actors galore,
Each splash tells a joke, always leaving us wanting more.

Tales from Fractured Shores

The tide brings in tales, a funny old crew,
With a sardine who sings in a fishy-toe shoe.
He struts on the sand with a shell as his mic,
While clam shells do giggles, oh what a hike!

A dolphin named Chuckles flips with a cheer,
While crabs try to laugh but don't know how to steer.
They scuttle and tumble, a comical sight,
As waves tickle toes in a magical night.

Then a starfish declares with a wink and a grin,
"I'll tell you the secrets of where humor begins!"
But before he can start, he's pulled by the tide,
And we all burst out laughing, unable to hide.

So listen up close as the sea writes its script,
For life in the ocean is wild and well-equipped.
With echoes of laughter, they shimmer and play,
In fractured shores where the funny fish stay.

The Nonchalant Drift

Drifting through currents, a fish with no care,
Said, "Life's just a swim, you wouldn't believe where!"
He met a lazy turtle who yawned on a log,
And joked about how he was late for a fog.

The pufferfish puffed up on discovering fun,
"I'm not round, I'm just here under the sun!"
They giggled at snails, so slow and so shy,
Who were racing for pearls, oh my, oh my!

A snapper tried laughing; it came out a snap,
While starfish flipped stories, their five-finger clap.
The clownfish, of course, kept cracking the jokes,
"Bubbles and chuckles, oh what do I soak?"

With seaweed swaying, in breezy delight,
They drifted together until it was night.
The moon winked above, in its silvery mist,
And all in the sea couldn't help but persist.

Murmurs of the Sea

The murmurs arise, from the depths of the blue,
Where a flounder named Fred cracked jokes that were true.
He said, "Why do seapeople love a good pun?
Because it's all about laughter under the sun!"

A whale might just chime in, hum a sweet tune,
"I'm big but I'm funny, not just a balloon!"
With dolphins who somersault, dancing in rings,
The ocean erupts as the laughter it brings.

A shoal of sardines make quite the parade,
While jellyfish jiggle, to some beats that they played.
With ticklish sea cucumbers, don't take them for shy,
For when they get laughing, they'll reach for the sky!

So come, join the fun in these wild ocean tales,
Where every ripple's comedy, singing through sails.
In the depths of this water, where giggles run free,
You'll find that the humor flows endlessly.

Streams of Whispered Wishes

In a pond where the frogs like to chat,
A fish pondered life, wearing a hat.
He'd wave at the ducks, so bold and spry,
While dreaming of soaring, oh me, oh my!

With bubbles of laughter and splashes of fun,
He raced with the turtles, but they just shun.
"I'm the fastest!" he'd boast with a flip of his tail,
As they glided past, leaving him to wail!

He spun in circles, a dizzying swirl,
While minnows all giggled and gave him a twirl.
"Just wait 'til I grow!" he'd yell with delight,
But they'd just swim off, giggling in flight.

So here's to the fish with the whimsical dream,
In waters where silliness flows like a stream.
For every splash tells a funny old fable,
Of a fish and his hopes, all glad and unstable!

The Coral Crown's Lament

Down where the corals wear crowns made of shells,
A crab gave a speech that no one repels.
"I'm king of the reef, with a royal decree,
But these fish just keep laughing; oh woe is me!"

With an air of importance, he strutted around,
But his crown slipped and fell, rolling onto the ground.
The clownfish all chuckled, the starfish all sighed,
As they watched their old ruler's majestic slide.

He scratched at his claws, with a humorous pout,
"Now listen here, folks, you'll see what I'm about!
I'm still the best crab; you'll come to agree,
Once I find my old crown, just wait and you'll see."

So he searched high and low, in the sand and the rocks,
While the fish threw a party in their bright socks.
"Come join us," they sang, "let's make it a blast!"
And the crab couldn't help but laugh at the past.

Mysteries of the Underwater Globe

In a world filled with bubbles, where secrets abound,
A fish told a story that echoed around.
"Have you heard of the treasure beneath the waves?"
But his friends just rolled eyes and said, "You're so dazed!"

"It's shiny and golden, with jewels all aglow,
And guarded by seaweed and one grumpy crow!"
The seahorse laughed loud, "You tell quite a tale,
Last week you said it was chased by a whale!"

Yet our fish pushed on, with a grin on his face,
Drawing maps with his fins in a whimsical race.
The others just smiled, with a twinkle of glee,
Heartfelt with joy for their friend, oh so free.

So they swam through the currents, together in cheer,
With dreams of adventures, there's nothing to fear.
For amidst all the legends, they found what was true,
The laughter of friendship, that sparkly blue!

Ballad of the Floating Isles

On floating isles where the seaweed grows tall,
Lived weird little critters, the funniest of all.
With snail-based musical chairs on hand,
They danced 'round the lilies in their wacky band.

The fish would all bubble, mouths wide with surprise,
As crabs did the tango, flashing their thighs!
"Who knew that you danced?" a goldfish exclaimed,
While one crab just blushed; he was feeling quite famed.

The air was alive with a melody bright,
As sea stars twinkled with joy through the night.
The angelfish giggled, like notes in the breeze,
As they spun with the rhythm, confident with ease.

With laughter and fun in their bubbling pool,
These critters discovered there's magic in cool.
So come round and join in the party's delight,
For the floating isles are a wonderful sight!

Currents of Connection

In the river, a fish named Lou,
Grew gills that glimmered and shone bright blue.
He told all the tales, oh what a sight,
Of dancing with frogs in the moonlight.

With a flip and a splash, he would say,
'Join me, my friends, it's a fishy ballet!'
The turtles would chuckle, the otters would grin,
As they joined the parade with a splash and a spin.

One day a catfish, with whiskers so long,
Tried to join in but slipped and was gone,
Bubble-blowing laughter echoed so wide,
As Lou swam around with triumph and pride.

Fishy connections made by the stream,
Where laughter flowed freely, it seemed like a dream.
With scales gleaming bright under the sun,
In the currents of joy, they all had such fun!

The Serenity of the Still Pond

In a pond so quiet, where the lilies swayed,
Lived a goldfish named Gary, who always displayed,
A penchant for jokes that would tickle the soul,
But his best friend, a frog, found it hard to console.

Gary declared, 'Let's have a grand show,
With fishy slapstick, and splashes to throw!'
The frogs croaked along, their voices all mixed,
As they choreographed jumps that left them all fixed.

One leap turned a splash, what a mess they did make,
With flies flying high, and a slippery cake.
They laughed as they tumbled, not a moment too soon,
With water ballet under the watch of the moon.

So there in the stillness, they danced with such zest,
In a world made for fun, they felt truly blessed.
With giggles and splashes marking the night,
In waters so calm, everything felt right.

Breaths of the Sea

In the ocean waves, with a whole lot of cheer,
A dolphin named Dash spread laughter so clear.
He'd flip and he'd splash, oh what a delight,
With whale friends around, they played day and night.

Each morning they'd gather, a quirky parade,
With octopuses juggling, a splashy charade.
The sea turtles would giggle, the crabs clapped along,
In the salty sea breeze, they felt so strong.

One day a sardine tried to join in the fun,
But slipped on a jelly and fell with a thun!
Curling in laughter, they welcomed the blunder,
In their underwater world, they'd always find wonder.

With waves full of joy and bubbles of bliss,
In an ocean of laughter, you can't help but miss,
The wacky adventures that each day would bring,
In a sea full of friends, they'd always take wing!

Whims of the Water Dancers

In a river of whims where the current did sway,
The minnows were laughing, oh what a play!
They twirled with the leaves, they spun with the breeze,
Dancing in circles with such perfect ease.

A plucky little fish with a glint in his eye,
Announced with a splash, 'Let's see who can fly!'
The water was rippling, the frogs jumped with glee,
As fish made the moves of a wild jubilee.

But along came a heron, so tall and so sly,
He swiped at the minnows and made a big try.
But instead of panic, the fish did a twist,
And right in that moment, the heron was missed!

With bubbles of laughter rising up from below,
The river rejoiced in their rhythmic flow.
So here in the water, with friends all around,
The whimsy of dancing was truly profound!

Secrets of the Coral Kingdom

In the coral castle, whispers roam,
A crab plays king on a sandy throne.
He tickles the seaweed, they giggle and sway,
While the clownfish blush when the octopus plays.

Dancing with bubbles, a sea slug shouts,
A party of fish swims, laughing about.
The porcupine puffer pretends to be shy,
While the curious seahorse just winks with one eye.

A turtle tells tales of jellyfish pranks,
As shrimp on the sidelines offer their thanks.
"More laughs, more bubbles!" they chant with great cheer,

The coral's secret? It's fun all year!

So next time you dive and you hear giggling sounds,
Remember the kingdom where humor abounds.
In the dance of the waves, let joy take the lead,
For the coral's bright secrets are all that you need.

Fins and Fables

Once a fish with fins so bright,
Danced with seaweed in morning light.
He spun and twirled, oh what a sight,
While a starfish laughed with all its might.

A turtle, wise with tales and tricks,
Once raced a crab and called it quick.
But the crab just snickered, took a dip in muck,
Left the turtle wondering, 'What the...? How luck!'

The seahorses held a limbo affair,
With each bend and twist, they filled the air.
The grouper giggled, "You call that a move?"
And each little fish found their own funky groove.

With fins all shaking, the ocean turned bright,
Tales of the sea brought laughter at night.
In the depths where stories do mix and swirl,
Funny fables of friends make the ocean whirl.

Navigating the Blue

In waters so deep, where the sea cucumbers roam,
A guppy once dreamed of finding a home.
With a map made of bubbles and a heart full of glee,
He lost his way but found laughter with me!

A jellyfish floated, all wobbly and proud,
She glowed in the dark, attracting a crowd.
But a sardine quipped, "What's so special, dear light?"
And the jellyfish blushed, disappearing from sight!

A dolphin in search of a snazzy new hat,
Planned a big heist with a surfboarded brat.
"Oh, what fun!" they squealed, in a splashy chime,
Till the seaweed got tangled, and it all took time!

Yet in the blue depths, joy made its way,
Navigating smiles, come what may.
In tides of laughter, we swim and we glide,
For the ocean's our canvas, with humor our guide.

A Splash of Stories

One day a flounder tried to go straight,
But with eyes on the sides, he just couldn't relate.
He flipped and he flopped, what a silly dance,
As starfish stood guard, laughing at his chance!

A parrotfish grinned, changed colors galore,
With each little laugh, the waters would roar.
"Look at me change like a chameleon,
You can't catch my style, I'm a unique sea peon!"

A pufferfish pouted, "I'm way more than spines,
I tell the best jokes, just read the lines."
He puffed out his cheeks, then fell with a pop,
With giggles and bubbles, he could never stop!

So gather around, with shells and with sand,
For oceanic stories, let's make a fun band.
With laughter a-splashing and tales to explore,
In the depths of the sea, there's always much more!

www.ingramcontent.com/pod-product-compliance
Lightning Source LLC
Chambersburg PA
CBHW060137230426
43661CB00003B/462